T0007586

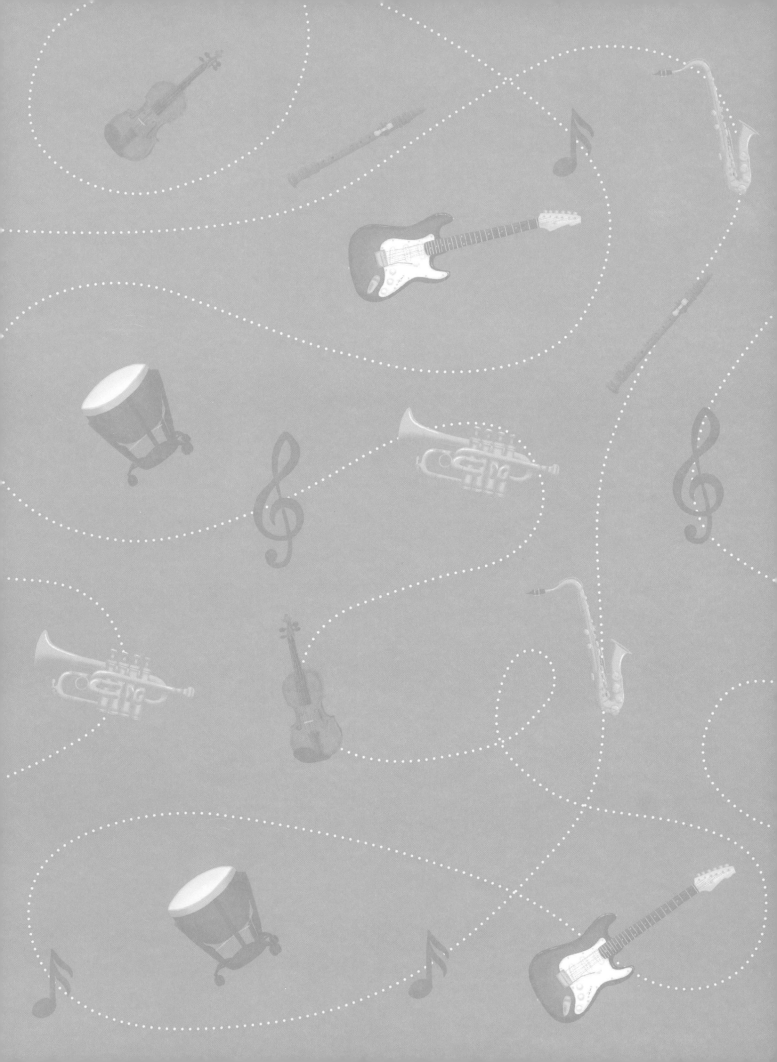

THE STORIES OF
MUSICAL
INSTRUMENTS

ŠTĚPÁNKA SEKANINOVÁ & JAKUB CENKL

ALBATROS

INTRODUCTION

"Tam-ta-da-daa! Tiddly, tiddly, tiddly, fiddly, middly, boom, boom, boom ..." Do you hear it? What a racket! Niccolo the cricket is bashing saucepans, banging lids, whistling, and altogether making quite a noise as he tries to coax out the notes of his favorite song. Big people and small, cover your ears, because this really isn't working out for Niccolo. What he needs are proper musical instruments and a bit of practice. That's right—a little more practice.

THE URGE TO PLAY

Crickets have six legs. They are said to have six tastes, too—and maybe there is some truth in that. With his six limbs, Niccolo has six times the appetite to become a musician. Just imagine him holding an instrument in each little foot, children! He would form a whole band on his own. And that is Niccolo's dream.

AN EAR FOR MUSIC

It may not seem so to you, but Niccolo has a musical ear. What is a musical ear, then? If you have one, you can distinguish whether a certain note is higher or lower, weaker or stronger. For singers and players of musical instruments, a musical ear is a real blessing.

LUCIANO THE SINGER

Niccolo's best friend is Luciano the nightingale. A rather inconspicuous bird at first sight, when he opens his little beak and sings, before long there is not a dry eye in the house. In short, Luciano has a golden voice. And what an accolade that is! It means that he has a great gift for singing, a lovely voice, and a musical ear.

My so-o-o-ong to you-u-u!

WHAT IS MUSIC?

Music is any sound or set of sounds that evoke feelings in us. For music to be music, we should **discover these four elements in it:**

Rhythm—the regular alternation of long and short tones and rests (playing a drum is an example of rhythm)
Melody—a sequence of notes linked to one another to express a musical idea (birdsong is an example of melody)
Harmony—a consonance and concord of tones in music (e.g., chords played on a piano or guitar)
Tone color—also known as timbre

MUSICAL INSTRUMENTS

Anything that produces sound is in essence a musical instrument. So the saucepans Niccolo bashes with a wooden spoon are musical instruments, too. But you must admit that the piano or the violin is more pleasing to the ear. Let's join Niccolo and Luciano on a quest to find the most beautiful instruments and the loveliest melodies!

CONTENTS

What would you like me to play?

PIANO
KEYBOARD INSTRUMENTS

Attracted by music soft and gentle, then wild and turbulent, Niccolo and Luciano have crept into the concert hall through the window. The notes are being played by a huge shiny black instrument that stands in the middle of the hall. On a stool next to the instrument sits a slim man in a tailcoat, his long fingers racing up and down the black and white keys. The man and the piano make beautiful music together.

INTRODUCING THE PIANO
The piano is one of the most voluminous musical instruments. It is an acoustic stringed instrument. When it is played, its strings vibrate when struck by wooden hammers attached to its 88 black and white keys. The white keys represent whole tones, the black keys semitones.

CONCERT GRAND PIANO

If you like, children, you can sing along with my playing.

MEET THE PIANO
Niccolo knows from the first that he must have this instrument in his band. Once again, Luciano's well-tuned voice sings along to the melody without a single wrong note. Children, allow me to present the concert grand piano.

THE STRINGS ARE ARRANGED VERTICALLY.

IT WILL EVEN FIT IN A SMALL APARTMENT.

UPRIGHT PIANO

Unlike the magnificent grand piano, you will find an upright piano in many a room and apartment. Standing smartly against a wall, it is the faithful servant of all beginning musicians. Because of its smaller size, the strings of an upright piano are arranged vertically in separate planes in order to fit them all in. The bass strings of an upright piano are thicker and shorter than those of a grand, giving the upright a more booming but narrower and less expansive tone.

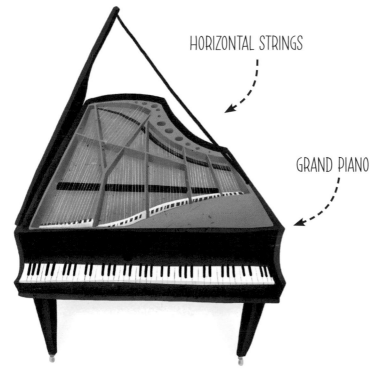

HORIZONTAL STRINGS

GRAND PIANO

GRAND PIANO

In terms of its shape, the grand piano looks like an outstretched bird's wing. This delights Luciano, and he struts around it and preens himself to show how proud he is. Because of its great size, it is more suitable for the concert hall than a small apartment—not just because it wouldn't fit into the apartment, but because its rich sound would be too much for a small space.

WHERE DOES THE WORD "PIANO" COME FROM?

The original name of the instrument, "pianoforte," makes plain that the whole dynamic scale is available to the player— from piano (soft) to forte (loud). This was not the case with the harpsichord, the forerunner of the piano.

Higher, higher!

DISTANT TONES FROM PREHISTORY

Isn't it incredible that the roots of the piano reach all the way back to prehistoric times? But the prehistoric piano was nothing luxurious, nor remotely similar to the modern-day piano. The piano's most distant ancestor was an ordinary stick. More specifically, it was a hollow stem of bamboo with a plant fiber cut into its top. The note produced by this primitive resonating instrument was neither impressive nor long-lasting.

HUMAN HAIR OR HORSEHAIR

Later, human hair, horsehair, or animal sinews were stretched across the bamboo stick. All these materials were better suited to music making than plant fiber, which was too fragile. Later still, in the 14th century, having experimented with silk thread, practical lovers of music came up with the metal string.

METAL STRINGS

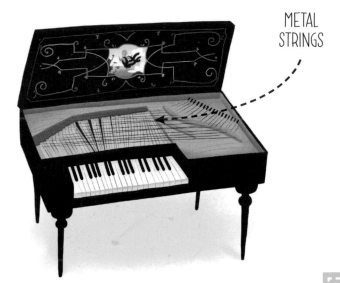

AND THEN THERE WAS THE CLAVICHORD …

Between the 12th and 14th centuries, the musical stick of prehistoric times was transformed. Following the tympanum and then the ancient monochord came the clavichord. The clavichord was a rectangular box on one side of which were between 20 and 22 keys. The keys on some clavichords shared strings—these were called fretted or gebunden—the player of such an instrument had to take care not to press two or more keys connected to the same string.

Laa-laa-aa! Faster!

GLORY BE! THE PIANO IS BORN!

It happened in the early 18th century. The happy father was Bartolomeo Cristofori, an Italian maker of musical instruments and custodian of the musical instruments of the famous Medici family. The hammers of his offspring produced softer and louder tones, as the player required. He called it a "stromento col piano e forte."

> **!** **PROS OF THE CLAVICHORD:** SMALLNESS MAKES IT EASY TO STORE; IT COULD **BE PLACED** ON A TABLETOP.
> **CONS OF THE CLAVICHORD:** WEAK, LACKLUSTRE SOUND.

LONG LIVE THE MODERN WORLD!

If Bartolomeo Cristofori were to return to the world today, how surprised he would be! The first electric pianos went into production in the second half of the 20th century. These instruments mimic the sound of the acoustic piano, but they do so electronically, not by vibrating strings. One advantage of an electric piano is that it doesn't need to be tuned.

> **!** **IN THE 19TH CENTURY,** MANY MORE IMPROVEMENTS WERE MADE TO **THE PIANO.** BY THE END OF THAT CENTURY, IT HAD BECOME THE INSTRUMENT **WE KNOW TODAY.**

A GLASS PIANO? SERIOUSLY?

Yes, really! Some pianos and piano makers are eccentric. At the beginning of the 21st century, Canada's Heintzman & Co. produced the super-deluxe Heintzman Crystal Grand, which was made of crystal. Niccolo longed to play it, but there was no chance of that—there is only one such instrument in the whole world! Another famous piano is the one played by John Lennon of the Beatles. Lennon composed many world-famous songs on this instrument, and he loved it so much that it moved with him from studio to studio.

CRYSTAL PIANO

I have to be careful, it's fragile.

LENNON'S PIANO

FRANZ LISZT

This Hungarian musician, composer and conductor, who lived from 1811 to 1886, was a true virtuoso of the piano. It is said that the Norwegian composer Edvard Grieg once went to Liszt with his Piano Concerto only to discover that he lacked the courage to play the most difficult part of his own composition. Liszt took the manuscript and played the passage straight away, without making a single mistake.

A pianist's fingers are really important.

SERGEI RACHMANINOFF

FRÉDÉRIC CHOPIN

This virtuoso of the piano, who lived from 1810 to 1849, was such a brilliant player of his instrument that he earned the nickname "poet of the piano." How many musicians write their first compositions at seven years of age? Well, Chopin did. How many musicians enchant concert audiences at such a young age? Chopin was one such, for sure. It will come as no surprise to learn that this Polish genius was considered a new Mozart.

FRÉDÉRIC CHOPIN

That's what I call setting the bar high!

FRANZ LISZT

SERGEI RACHMANINOFF

Sergei Rachmaninoff (1873–1943) was a famous Russian composer. Like Franz Liszt, he demonstrated a great musical gift in his sensitive, lively performances as well as in his compositions. Thanks to his remarkably long fingers, Rachmaninoff was able to play very difficult chords that ordinary musicians could never dream of playing.

SYMPHONY ORCHESTRA

An orchestra is a relatively large group of players of string, percussion, woodwind, and brass instruments led by a conductor. An ancestor of the orchestra is the small chamber ensemble, which became widespread in the 18th century.

BIG DRUM

GRAND PIANO

SECOND VIOLIN

FIRST VIOLIN

TRIANGLE

FRENCH HORN

TRUMPET

FLUTE

CLARINET

DOUBLE BASS

CELLO

POLYPHONIC INSTRUMENTS

KEYBOARD & WIND INSTRUMENTS

POLYPHONIC

"Do you hear that angelic music? Have we arrived in paradise?" Niccolo let himself be carried away on the fine threads of a tender melody, dreaming of the heavens. "That's an organ," Luciano the nightingale explained to the cricket. "A wonderful, regal musical instrument." And also one of the largest and most complex.

Whew, it is so heavy!

JIGSAW PUZZLE

An organ is no simple matter. Only the very best instrument makers are able to build one. It requires real talent to put so many components together in the creation of something so amazing. The building of an organ is a combination of art and craft. In terms of its construction, it is the most complicated of all musical instruments. While some organs are quite small, others are huge. Nowhere in the world will you find two organs that are identical in terms of their construction, appearance, size, and sound! Each organ is made to measure for a particular space. Organists can never know exactly what to expect from an instrument, so they must familiarize themselves with it before they start playing. This is very different from the experience of violinists, who always play their own instrument and take it everywhere with them. Did you know that an organ is played with the hands and the feet? Here, you can see for yourself all the things that go together to make up this amazing instrument. To describe an organ in every detail would need a whole book, however.

PROSPECT

What we see of an organ at first sight—the decorative façade of its case comprising the pipes—is known as its prospect. The prospect is usually designed to suit the architecture of its surroundings, in most cases a church. The prospect may include mute pipes, which are merely decorative, as well as playing pipes.

ORGAN CASE

The organ case contains the organ mechanism. It protects this mechanism from dust and sunlight, as well as protecting the instrument from unauthorized playing.

TRACKER ACTION

The tracker action refers to the mechanical linkage of the keys or the register on the console with the pipes.

WIND CHEST

Put simply, this is the wooden chest under the pipes, into which air is fed through the air reservoir and which contains valves controlled by the player by means of the console. The pressing of a key by the organist opens a valve in the wind chest, releasing air to the pipe, thus producing the sound.

Do you hear that heavenly music?

PIPES

ORGAN MECHANISM

The main part of the organ mechanism is the wind chest, with its series of pipes that produce the instrument's sound. A flow of air is fed to the pipes from ventilators to the bellows, and from there through the air reservoir to the wind chest under the pipes.

PIPES

The pipes produce the organ's sound. There are many kinds of pipes, some made of wood, some metal. Wooden pipes are mostly spruce. Metal pipes are made of an alloy of tin and lead, or of zinc and copper. There are many kinds of pipes, including flue, reed, tube, conical, open, half-open, and closed. ("So many that it's making my head spin!" said Niccolo.)

REGISTER

A register is a series of pipes with a certain tonal quality. In creating the instrument's sound, a register can be used on its own or in combination with other registers.

TUNING AN ORGAN

An organ, too, must be kept in tune. All organ pipes are tuned as part of the production process and from time to time after that. Reed pipes, which are very sensitive to changes in temperature, need to be tuned most often.

PROSPECT

CONSOLE

ORGAN CASE

CONSOLE

The console comprises a keyboard for the hands and a pedalboard for the feet. Sometimes, even when the organ is switched on, air is flowing into it, and the organist is pressing the keys, still the instrument may be silent. How come? Well, for the organ to play, it is necessary for the organist to switch on one or more registers on the console.

EXTRA EQUIPMENT

For organs of all sizes, there is a lot of extra equipment to help with playing, such as shutters, fixed combinations, pistons, crescendo pedal, and setzer.

WATER OR AIR?

The organ has a long history. The very first one was built in 240 BCE by a man named Ctesibius. As he was very fond of his wife Thais, he taught her how to play the new instrument. So, now you know the name of the world's first woman organist, too. All this took place in ancient Greece. The organ of that time was much smaller than today's instrument, and the air was blown into it by a water pump. It is known as a hydraulis (water organ).

THAIS

WATER ORGAN

! ROMAN LEGIONARIES HAD THEIR OWN ORGANIST. **FIGHTING WAS EASIER TO THE SOUND OF AN ORGAN.**

COME ON YOU GLADIATORS!

In ancient Rome, palace banquets were held to the sound of organ music. It was also heard at the theater, the Roman circus, chariot races, and even notorious gladiator fights. Emperor Nero may be known for his cruelty, but he was also an enthusiastic organist. It is said that one night Nero had all his senators brought from their beds so that he could show them how well he played.

SMALL, LARGE, TINY

No doubt you know that organs in the naves of cathedrals are magnificent in terms of both sound and size. There is no question of their crouching shyly in a corner. But both antiquity and the Middle Ages had portable organs known as portatives. The portative would hang from the performer's shoulder. He would play it with one hand and use the other to blow air to the pipes.

PORTATIVE

EMPEROR NERO

What a strange way to build an organ!

There's a splendid view from here!

ORGAN RECORDS

LARGEST CHURCH ORGAN

The largest church organ is in St Stephen's Cathedral in Passau, Germany. I'm sure you will agree that 17,974 pipes are more than enough! This organ is also the largest in Europe and the fifth largest in the world. Not only is it beautiful to look at; it is still playable, allowing leading organists to coax heavenly music from it.

LARGEST ORGAN

The world's largest organ is in the Atlantic City Convention Hall. It has an incredible 33,112 pipes.

OLDEST ORGAN

It is thought that the organ in the church of Notre Dame de Valère in Sion, Switzerland, is the oldest playable organ in the world. This musical granny was born in the early 15th century.

MIDDLE AGES

In the Middle Ages, organ music accompanied secular pleasures. Today, however, we associate it with religious worship. How did this change happen, bearing in mind that the church at first looked down its nose at the organ? Well, only an organ could project its sound throughout the vast space of a Romanesque basilica or a Gothic cathedral.

DIFFERENT STROKES FOR DIFFERENT FOLKS

As the Middle Ages progressed, organs developed characteristics typical of where they were built. In Spain, for instance, some organ pipes reached out joyously into space. In England, this king of the instruments had no pedals.

OLDEST ORGAN

! IN THE BAROQUE ERA, THE ORGAN CAME INTO ITS OWN. HUGE CONCERTS WERE HELD WITH **THE ORGAN AS THE MAIN INSTRUMENT.** IN THE ROMANTIC ERA, ORGANS WERE BUILT IN CONCERT HALLS TOO, **MAKING THEM EVEN MORE POPULAR.**

JOHANN
SEBASTIAN BACH

JOHANN SEBASTIAN BACH

On hearing the word "organ," many of us think first of
Johann Sebastian Bach (1685–1750). Bach was a virtuoso
organist, a leading expert on what the organ could do,
and a brilliant composer of organ music. He played the
king of the instruments from a very young age, and he
loved to show off his skills in concerts. According to many
contemporary eyewitnesses, he had flawless keyboard
technique and was able to play from practically any notation
put in front of him. It is said that Bach was able to play with
his feet what many a proficient pianist could not even play
with their hands. As he was such a lover of the organ, it will
perhaps come as no surprise to learn that in the course of
his life Bach composed hundreds of works for the organ to
the glory of God. He was also a master musician on other
instruments, notably the violin.

FRANZ
LISZT

FRANZ LISZT

Franz Liszt (1811–1886), who was active in Austria-
Hungary, was a true virtuoso of the piano. From the piano,
it is but a small step to the organ—an instrument he
admired from the bottom of his gentle soul. Although the
organ was very much associated with church music, Liszt
wished for it to be played to express emotional experience,
not only to the glory of God. It was the same with his
compositions for the piano.

ACCORDION

"What's playing that beautiful, plaintive
music?" Niccolo wanted to know. It was
an accordion, of course! Although it may
not look like one, the accordion is a wind
instrument. It is also polyphonic. Air is
blown into the accordion not from the
mouth but by the expanding
and compressing of a
special bellows and the
pressing of buttons or
keys. Some accordions
have keyboards,
others buttons.

CAMERON
CARPENTER

CAMERON CARPENTER

Further proof that the organ belongs outside of
church is provided by young American organist
Cameron Carpenter (born 1981), whose portable
organ goes all over the world with him. Not only
does Carpenter perform the music of the old
masters; he plays his own compositions. This
gifted young man has played on the king of the
instruments since he was four years old. Thanks
to this combination of talent and hard work, he
has grown up to be an organ superstar.

BABY OF THE FAMILY

The accordion is a very young instrument. A forerunner of the accordion, known as the Handäoline, was made in 1822 by Berliner Friedrich Buschmann. The true accordion was patented in 1829 by Viennese instrument maker Cyrill Demian; it was indeed called the accordion, and it had several buttons. Today, the accordion is sometimes referred to as the squeezebox.

GREAT-GREAT-GRANDFATHER OF THE ACCORDION

Although the accordion is a baby among musical instruments, it can boast a great-great-grandfather. This is the sheng, which originated in China in the middle of the 1st millennium BCE. The sheng was composed of a bundle of seventeen bamboo pipes of different lengths and a body with a mouthpiece for the player to blow into.

SHENG

KEYBOARD

BELLOWS

BASS PART

PARTS OF THE ACCORDION

KEYBOARD
The static, melody-playing part is played with the right hand.

BELLOWS
The middle part, called the bellows, is for the pumping of air.

BASS PART
The accompanying bass part is played with the left hand.

HELLO WORLD!

The accordion immediately established itself in most places in Europe. It became so popular in urban surroundings that it was soon an integral part of urban folklore. Once the accordion's pleasing tones had conquered Europe, the instrument ventured across the great pond to North America.

! IN FINLAND, THE **ACCORDION IS CONSIDERED** A NATIONAL INSTRUMENT. JUST IMAGINE!

PAN FLUTE

The pan flute is a set of pipes attached to each other and contained in a special case. To make the instrument easier to play, the pipes are set in a slight arc.

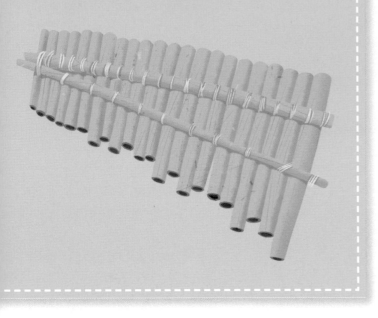

PAN

SYRINX

A HINT OF LEGEND

Once upon a time in ancient Greece, there was a god called Pan, who was half-man, half-goat. All day, every day, he would fly over the pastures, keeping a watchful, protective eye on the shepherds and their flocks. But then he met a beautiful nymph and fell madly in love with her. The nymph didn't care for the god Pan, however. Rather than marry him, she chose to become a reed at the riverside. But Pan loved her so much that he fashioned a flute from lengths of hollow reed and poured out all his sorrow and desire when playing it.

DIFFERENT PAN FLUTES

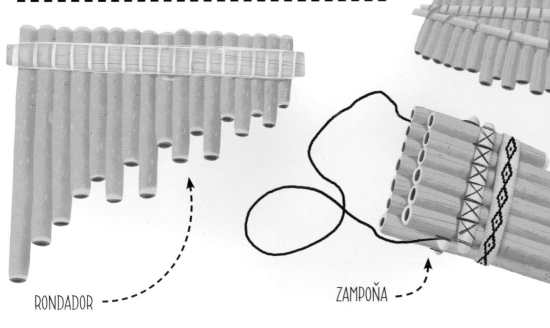

RONDADOR

ZAMPOŇA

ANTARA

! AS THE NYMPH LOVED **BY THE GOD PAN WAS CALLED SYRINX,** THE PAN FLUTE IS SOMETIMES **KNOWN BY THAT NAME.**

HISTORY

The pan flute is one of the world's oldest musical instruments, with a history that goes all the way back to the Stone Age—when it was made of reed, bamboo, cane, and hollow animal bone. Over time, simple pan flutes were adapted to the places where they were made.

HISS, HISS-SS-SS

The pan flute makes a hissing sound. It can faithfully imitate sounds of the breeze, the howling wind, and the natural world in general. Perhaps this explains its great popularity with indigenous peoples of South America. Hiss-ss, shoo-oo-mm, hiss-ss ...

SHOOOM

HISSSSSSSS

POPULARITY OF THE PAN FLUTE

You would be wrong to think that the pan flute is an instrument good enough for street musicians but nothing more. Not only is it popular all over the world, but there are concerts for pan flute at which famous flautists appear. Many of these players are Dutch. Yes, the land of clogs and tulips really loves the pan flute.

Nothing beats the pan flute!

CARINA BOSSENBROEK

Although the original pan flautist was the lovesick god Pan, mortals, too, are attracted by the instrument's plaintive tones. It comes as no surprise to see a talented young woman such as Carina Bossenbroek (born 1993), who fell for the instrument when she was just nine years old, performing in concert halls all over the world.

MATTHIJS KOENE

Matthijs Koene (born 1977) from the Netherlands is a true master of the pan flute. Not only has he won many important international awards for his playing; thanks to his brilliant technique, power of expression, and mastery of his instrument, he has opened the world of classical music to the simple pan flute.

Carina, could you teach me?

! **ALTHOUGH THE STRUCTURE** OF THE PAN FLUTE IS VERY SIMPLE, IT IS POSSIBLE **TO PLAY ALMOST ANYTHING ON IT—FROM BAROQUE MUSIC** TO MUSIC TAILOR-MADE FOR THE FLUTE AND **FOLK SONGS.**

BOWED STRING INSTRUMENTS

VIOLIN & OTHERS

What was making those angelic tones? Niccolo and Luciano turned towards the pleasing sound. Their gaze stopped at a girl holding an elegant instrument under her chin, using a slim bow to coax out the subtle trills of a lovely composition. No wonder they speak of the violin as a prince among musical instruments!

> Does this bow need an arrow?

BOW

VIOLIN

BODY

SCROLL

NECK

WHAT IS A VIOLIN?

A violin is a bowed string instrument with a truly beautiful sound. As its tone is not one of the strongest, there are many violins in an orchestra to ensure that it is properly heard and not drowned out by the wind instruments. The violin has long been an important part of the classical tradition, especially in Europe.

BOW

The violin has four strings and is played with the bow. The bow is composed of a wooden stick with a ribbon of horsehair strung taut from end to end. In the past, a violin bow looked more like an archer's bow—indeed, this instrument of combat was an important inspiration in its creation. Professionals refer to movements of the bow across the strings as strokes.

A LITTLE ABOUT THE HISTORY OF THE BOW

The first bows originated in ancient times in India and Persia. The bow appeared in north Africa and Spain around the 6th century. From the 17th century or thereabouts, the bow became straighter as it became progressively more like the bow of today.

CONSTRUCTION OF A VIOLIN

A violin is composed around a sound box referred to as its body. The body comprises two wooden plates, with cutouts on each side in the shape of the letter 'C' providing clearance for the bow. The plates are joined by means of the rib garland. To the body of the violin is attached the neck, which is composed of the fingerboard and the carved, spiral-shaped end part, known as the scroll. The strings are tightened by means of tuning pegs, which pass over the bridge.

ORIGIN OF THE VIOLIN

RAVANAHATHA

The first and oldest stringed instrument, the ravanahatha, originated in India. It was based around a simple hollowed-out cylinder of sycamore wood and two gazelle-gut strings. It was played with a bow of bamboo cane.

RAVANAHATHA

REBAB

The ancestors of the violin include an Arabian instrument called the rebab. Unlike the ravanahatha, it was three-stringed. Pear-shaped, its upper plate had two sound slits. It was played with a simple reed bow.

REBAB

CRWTH

The crwth is an early medieval (6th-century) instrument. Initially, it was plucked and strummed by singers to accompany their song. In the 10th century, it was embellished with a bow. From then on, the musician would play four of its six strings with a bow and the bottom two with the thumb. The original crwth was the sacred instrument of Celtic bards.

CRWTH

GUITAR OR VIOLIN?

The violin is one of the most difficult musical instruments to play. Unlike the guitar, it has no frets, so the player must know exactly where to put the fingers in order to achieve the desired note. As they play, violinists must be able to fine-tune their notes with great precision. Whoever wishes to play the violin must have an excellent musical ear.

HOPPING AND SKIPPING TO THE VIELLE

The musical instrument known as the vielle is a lot like the violin. It was extremely popular in the Middle Ages. But not all vielles were the same. Indeed, every vielle was different, as each player made their own. Vielles varied in the number of strings and the materials used.

VIELLE

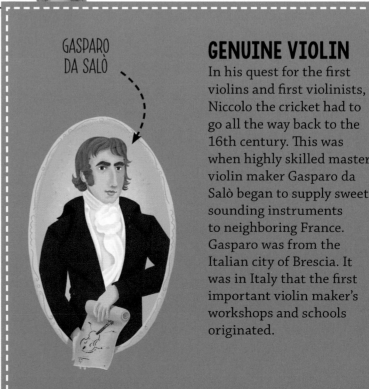

GASPARO DA SALÒ

GENUINE VIOLIN

In his quest for the first violins and first violinists, Niccolo the cricket had to go all the way back to the 16th century. This was when highly skilled master violin maker Gasparo da Salò began to supply sweet-sounding instruments to neighboring France. Gasparo was from the Italian city of Brescia. It was in Italy that the first important violin maker's workshops and schools originated.

WHAT EVERY VIOLIN MAKER DREAMS OF

The forest, that's what. In this regard, Niccolo the cricket and master violin makers are of like mind. The ideal is the special Stradivari forest in the Paneveggio national park in the Italian Alps, where the wood of spruces and maples has extraordinary properties of resonance. Antonio Stradivari discovered this by chance, having bought material for the making of violins from some woodcutters. Today, wood from Stradivari's forest is precious indeed.

GREATEST VIOLIN MAKER OF THEM ALL

The Italian Antonio Giacomo Stradivari has gone down in history as the most brilliant violin maker of them all. Having opened his workshop in the town of Cremona in 1680, he began his search for the secret of the perfect instrument. He tried various thicknesses of wood, experimented with different varnishes, and looked for new ways of building a violin. And his efforts paid off: Stradivarius violins are still regarded as the best in the world, and they are the most expensive.

VIOLINS BY STRADIVARI

I'll take all three, please!

ANTONIO STRADIVARI WORKED AS A VIOLIN MAKER **FROM THE AGE OF TWELVE.** HE PRODUCED ABOUT 2,000 UNIQUE INSTRUMENTS **IN HIS LIFETIME.**

ANTONIO VIVALDI

Antonio Lucio Vivaldi (1678–1741) was another Italian virtuoso of the violin. Rather than follow his father into the barber's trade, he became a priest, musician, and composer. His most popular work is *The Four Seasons*, four violin concerti each celebrating a different season in the countryside around Mantua, which Vivaldi loved so much.

ANTONIO VIVALDI

NICOLÒ PAGANINI

Let us introduce you to Nicolò Paganini (1782–1840), the most brilliant violinist of all time. A slim figure with long legs, long arms, and long fingers, he practiced hard from a very young age. Thanks to his extremely broad hand span and the suppleness of his fingers, he could play the apparently impossible. Some of his contemporaries even thought he had done a deal with the devil. But Paganini was about talent and hard work, not conjury.

NICOLÒ PAGANINI

My role model?
Well, Paganini
of course!

VANESSA MAE

"What a strange violin that woman is playing!" marveled Niccolo. Vanessa Mae (born Vanessa Mae Vanakorn, 1978) plays electric violins and acoustic ones. Electric violins have real clout! Vanessa Mae is a pretty progressive woman—she combines classical and pop music, and she races as an Alpine skier too!

THE CELLO
IS HELD BETWEEN
THE KNEES.

CELLO

At the time of the Renaissance and in the Baroque period, the viola da gamba was a very popular musical instrument. Held between the knees, it was played with a special bow across its six or seven strings. The violoncello (better known as the cello) originated in the 16th century, inspired by the shapes of the violin and the viola da gamba. There were two types, the larger for accompaniment, the smaller for solos.

SWEET VIOLET—THE VIOLA

The viola—which we might call the sister of the violin—has a magical, husky, mysterious sound. Not only is it larger and heavier than the violin, but its strings are thicker, meaning that it needs a more substantial bow than the violin. All this explains the viola's lovely, darker tone.

VIOLIN

THE VIOLA
IS BIGGER.

DOUBLE BASS

The double bass emerged in Italy from the bass viola da gamba at the same time as the violin—the 16th century. Although part of the orchestra at the court of Louis XIV, this instrument was not included in operatic and symphony orchestras until sometime in the 18th century. And considering its hugeness, it's no wonder! It is said that the bass gives the music a solid, deep-toned basis out of which to grow.

Aren't I too small for
the double bass?

BIG BAND

A big band is a large swing ensemble led not by a conductor but by one of the instrumentalists, known as the bandleader. The smallest big band comprises 17 musicians.

DOUBLE BASS

TROMBONE

DRUMS

CLARINET

BANDMASTER
WITH TRUMPET

23

PERCUSSION INSTRUMENTS

DRUM SET & PERCUSSION

Boom, boom, boom, ta-da-ta, boom, boom, boom . . . There was banging and beating coming from all sides. Poor, frightened Niccolo had to cover his delicate musical ears. "What's all this fighting and shooting? Is there a war going on?" he asked his singer friend. Luciano grinned from one side of his beak to the other. "It's only drumming! And percussion instruments have a very important place in music!"

BEATING A DRUM

Percussion instruments are among the very oldest musical instruments. Which figures, as even for our most distant ancestors, it was the easiest thing to beat, shake, or rattle something. It will come as no surprise to learn that there are probably more types of drums than any other musical instrument. Percussion instruments in a group are referred to as a set.

FROM TIME IMMEMORIAL

There were already drummers in prehistoric times. Clay drums with a membrane made of animal skin dating from the period around 3000 BCE have been found in Europe. This does not mean, of course, that there was no drumming before then—even older instruments have probably not survived because they were made of a perishable material, most notably wood.

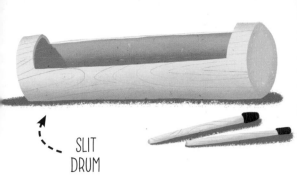

SLIT DRUMS

Slit drums are older still than classic membranophones (drums with skins). A slit drum comprises a hollow wooden barrel with a slit along its entire length, which the drummer beats with sticks.

SLIT DRUM

DRUMS FOR WOMEN ONLY

Drumming continued into ancient times. In Mesopotamia, barrel drums could have two heads or one. The sound of a two-headed frame drum was indispensable to festive rituals. Some of these drums were so large that they needed two players. And these drummers were women: in the ancient empire between the Euphrates and Tigris rivers, these sacred drums were played by women only.

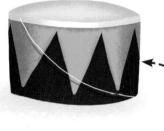

SNARE DRUM

Boom, boom, march, march!

SNARE DRUM

This high-bodied drum is distinguished by its dark, terrifying sound. In the Middle Ages, together with pipes, it was used to accompany soldiers on the march. It was also heard at places of execution. This drum was played just before something horrible happened.

SIDE DRUM

BASS DRUM

SIDE DRUM

A side drum, in olden times, was carried by parish constables, whose loud drumming would attract the attention of passers-by before an official declaration or announcement was read aloud. A side drum is played with two thin sticks of hard wood.

KETTLE DRUMS

Kettle drums stand on three legs and have quite a deep sound. Like most musical instruments, the kettle drum originated in Asia, first coming to the attention of Europeans during the Crusades. As well as being a military drum, the kettle was used in ceremonies at court. It became part of orchestras playing classical music around the middle of the 17th century.

(BIG) BASS DRUM

Also known as the Turkish drum or the giant drum, the bass drum is 30 inches in diameter and 20 inches high. It is played using a special pedal attached to a felt-covered mallet. It's hardly surprising that bass drums are popular in orchestras: a bass drum sounds great in combination with other bass instruments.

TIMPANI, OR KETTLE DRUM

TABLA

Traditional Indian tabla drums must always be played together. Before starting to play, the drummer must place them on special mats. The right hand plays the wooden daya drum, which has several layered skins, while the left produces bass tones on the metal baya drum. Both drums are played using a special finger technique.

DAYA DRUM

BAYA DRUM

BONGOS

These small, skin-covered drums with open bottoms are among the very oldest percussion instruments. Played with the hands, without sticks, the earliest mention of this distinctive instrument comes from eastern Cuba.

BONGOS

! PERCUSSION COMPRISES DRUMS, CYMBALS, STANDS, AND **OTHER INSTRUMENTS** THAT **ARE STRUCK,** SCRAPED, OR RUBBED.

CONGA

"No, no, Niccolo, those are drums called congas, not barrels!" laughed Luciano. "Though I must admit they do look like barrels. The conga, too, originated in Cuba. Learn how to strike its head with your palm and fingers and off you go. You can play salsa and jazz too."

CONGAS

NTAMA TALKING DRUM

More than anything, the body of this African drum looks like an hourglass. The player holds the drum in the curve of the arm, using the hand of that arm to produce notes by pressing on strings stretched across the sides of the instrument, while the other hand is striking the goat-skin head with a stick. The talking drum is used to summon people to meetings.

NTAMA

MANY DRUMS TOGETHER

A drum kit is many drums played together as a set. Drum kits originated in Great Britain in the early 18th century for a very simple reason: theaters had too little available space and too little money to engage more than one drummer. Nothing could be easier than to set up a drum kit for a single musician.

YOU CAN'T PLAY WITHOUT STICKS

"Why so many sticks?" asked Niccolo with amazement, as Luciano handed him a large bundle of them. "Why do you think?" replied Luciano, shaking his head. "If you beat your drums properly, your sticks will soon turn to splinters. No drummer turns up at a concert without a plentiful supply."

KEITH MOON

Perhaps the most famous drummer of all time is Keith Moon (1946–1978), nicknamed Nobby. Moon started playing drums when he was fourteen. Three years later, he became a full member of the band The Who. Moon's drumming was great to watch. Often, at the end of a concert, he would smash up his kit. On one occasion, he filled his drums with explosives, thus ending his performance with a grand exit. If he fancied goldfish in his drums, he simply filled them with water for that purpose. Nobby was a rock drummer to the very depths of his musical soul.

One won't be enough . . .

KEITH MOON

PARTS OF THE DRUM KIT

RIDE CYMBAL
Unlike the hi-hat, this resonates longer after it is struck with a stick and has more distinct sound.

FLOOR TOM
This lies on the floor, within easy reach.

TOM-TOMS
These are drums whose job is to connect one part of a song with another.

BASS DRUM
This is sometimes known as the big drum.

SNARE DRUM
This is also known as the small drum.

CRASH CYMBAL
On its own stand, this cymbal is struck with a wooden or felt stick. It rewards the player with its powerful, penetrative sound.

HI-HAT
Composed of a stand to which a pair of cymbals is attached horizontally, this is used to maintain the tempo.

RIDE CYMBAL

CRASH CYMBAL

TOM-TOMS

FLOOR TOM   BASS DRUM   SNARE DRUM   HI-HAT

HISTORY OF CYMBALS

Cymbals are of ancient, Oriental origin. The earliest known mentions of them are from Armenia, Mesopotamia, ancient Egypt, China, and India; later, they are known to have appeared in ancient Greece and Rome. It took a while for cymbals to catch on in Europe, however. They first attracted interest in the 17th century, when an army from the Ottoman Empire invaded Europe. At first, cymbals were part of the bass drum, allowing the player to drum with a stick in one hand and smack the cymbal held in his other hand against a cymbal attached to the drum.

CYMBALS

CAJÓN

This box, too, is a musical instrument. It is called a cajón. No wonder it looks like a shipping crate: after they were forced to burn their own instruments, slaves made the first cajóns from boxes used for the transportation of fish and fruit. To play the cajón, you must sit with your legs on either side of it and use your hands to beat on its front and sides.

CAJÓN

CLACK, CLACK, CASTANETS

In the beginning, in the Asia of ancient times, there were two flat shells. When tapped together, these shells kept great rhythm. Later, rather than searching for the right kind of shells, musicians were able to make their own castanets—from bone, horn, or, more commonly, wood. They came to Europe with the Arabian Moors. The Spanish immediately adopted them as their own. Can you imagine Spanish flamenco dancing without castanets? I can't.

SO HOW ARE CASTANETS PLAYED?

This instrument's two little bowls are joined at their protrusions by a string. The musician or dancer puts the string over the thumb and moves the fingers to the rhythm. The movement of the fingers causes the bowls to knock against each other, producing a lovely, distinctive clacking sound.

I'm dancing with you!

Hop off, Niccolo, or I'll give you a tinkle.

TRIANGLE

HOW MANY ANGLES?

You would be forgiven for thinking that the triangle has ancient origins. But this delicate percussion instrument wasn't even always a triangle; before it became one, it had as many as eight angles! Like the cymbals, the triangle was spread across Europe by the music of the Janissaries of the Ottoman army. The triangle is nothing more than a thick metal bar bent into a triangular shape. Whenever it is tapped by a metal beater, it produces a clear, bright note.

CELESTA

PIANO OR PERCUSSION?

"Is it a piano or not?" said Niccolo, scratching his head over a strange, sturdy, many-keyed instrument. "It's not a piano, it's a celesta," Luciano explained. In an orchestra, however, it is played by a professional pianist, even though it is part of the percussion family. The word "celesta" means "heavenly." It is played by hammers that strike metal strips, producing delicate chime-like sounds. A relatively young instrument, it was invented in the late 19th century. Russian composer Pyotr Ilyich Tchaikovsky liked the gentle sound of the celesta so much that it came to play an integral role in his compositions.

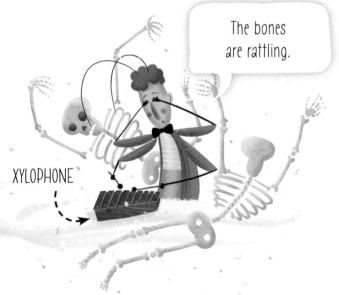

The bones are rattling.

XYLOPHONE

TUBULAR BELLS

If you're looking for a musical instrument called tubular bells, don't expect to find something pear-shaped. These are hollow tubes of metal of various lengths, attached to a special frame. When the player hits them with a hammer, they sound like real bells.

XYLOPHONE

This is a row of rectangular wooden bars of different lengths, struck by mallets of wood, rubber, or plastic. The shorter the bar, the higher the note the xylophone produces. This pleasing instrument comes from southeast Asia and Africa; it didn't arrive in Europe until the 15th century. It was first played by an orchestra in Camille Saint-Saens' *Danse Macabre*, where it represents the sound of rattling bones.

DR-R-RUM, DR-R-RUM

"All this drumming, banging, and ringing is giving me a headache. But now I know for sure that my band can't get by without percussion. Anyway, it's time to move on and find out about more instruments. I don't want to miss a single one!"

BRASS INSTRUMENTS
WIND INSTRUMENTS

"Ta-rum-ta-da-daa, ta-rum-ta-da-daa!" So "sang" a gleaming trumpet in all directions. Niccolo stood with his cricket mouth agape, listening agog. The voice of Luciano the songbird complemented the instrument with high, melodious trills. "Well, I definitely want a trumpet in my orchestra!" thought Niccolo to himself. He just couldn't get enough of the sound of brass.

VALVES

BELL

MOUTHPIECE

INTRODUCING THE TRUMPET

The trumpet is a brass wind instrument. It is constructed of a brass tube bent in a rounded oblong shape, which is wider at its end. Through nearly-closed lips, a trumpet player blows a hefty dose of air into the mouthpiece, thus producing beautiful, high, full notes that find expression in most genres of music. The note played depends on the strength of the air blown.

TRUMPET TYPES

PICCOLO TRUMPET

POCKET TRUMPET

"Wow, how small that instrument is!" gushed Niccolo in amazement. "In fact, it would fit in my pocket!" Well, wouldn't you know, it's called a pocket trumpet! The 51-inch-long tube of this special instrument is wound so tightly that the instrument is only 8 inches in length.

AIDA TRUMPET

The Aida trumpet is the invention of the great composer Giuseppe Verdi. He needed it to play the triumphal march in his opera *Aida*. It is a narrow tube, which extends into a cone shape at its end.

PICCOLO TRUMPET

The piccolo trumpet is half the size of the standard trumpet, pitching it a whole octave higher.

POCKET TRUMPET

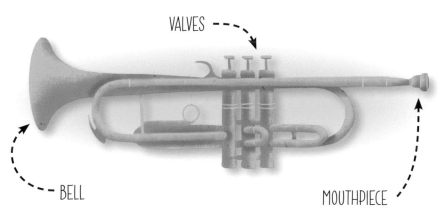

AIDA TRUMPET

BRASS IS THE MOST COMMON MATERIAL FROM WHICH **TRUMPETS ARE MADE.**

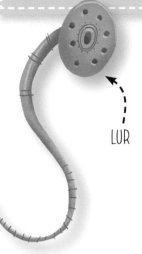

LUR

BRONZE AGE

Niccolo's ancestor from the Bronze Age is blowing hard on something. But what is it? That's right, it's an early trumpet. More specifically, it is an S-shaped metal instrument called a lur. This was played most often on ceremonial occasions.

How that elephant tusk hurts my ears!

PREHISTORIC TRUMPETERS

The history of the trumpet reaches all the way back to prehistoric times. Prehistoric trumpets weren't much like the trumpets of today, however. They were simply hollow animal horns, which our distant ancestors blew into with all their strength. They did this to scare away enemies or warn their tribe of danger. The sound this trumpet made was rough rather than smooth. The tusks of mammoths and elephants had the greatest effect.

ANTIQUITY

Ancient warriors are gathering for battle. The bright sound of trumpets carries to every ear. When battle is joined, the trumpets play on for all they are worth. "Have no fear! Shout and fight! You are the stronger!" sings the brass. That's right; in days of old, trumpets urged soldiers to ever greater feats of courage and ferocity.

SALPINX

SALPINX

The horn of the ancient Greeks was called the salpinx. There was nothing special about it: it was just an ordinary long tube that opened out at the end. But its sound served to make the heart feel bold.

BLOW YOUR HORN!

For the ancient Greeks, the horn called the salpinx and its mystical brass sound were so special that they competed in the Olympic Games! The winning players made the loudest noise or succeeded in holding their breath longer than the others. The stronger a player's lungs, the greater his chance of victory. It was reported that a certain Herodorus of Megara was the champion horn player in ten consecutive Olympic Games. Herodorus's lungs were so powerful that they could blow two salpinges at once.

OH MY GOD!

In ancient times, trumpets didn't only appear on the battlefield. Thanks to their wonderful, mysterious tone, they played an exceptional and important role in ceremonies dedicated to the gods, as a result of which they were long regarded as instruments of the higher classes. In those days, there wasn't even a trade in trumpets.

ROMANCE OF THE MIDDLE AGES

Can you imagine a knights' tournament without a blast of the trumpet to open it? Niccolo the cricket certainly can't! A tournament without a trumpet isn't a proper tournament. So the role of the trumpet in the Middle Ages is clear to us. But this was also the time of an all-powerful church, when the human voice was preferred to musical instruments. As a result, the trumpet development slowed for a while.

LONG LIVE THE TRUMPET!

The 17th century was a good time for the trumpet. Composers wrote music for it, and it found its rightful place in the orchestra. "Long live the trumpet!" cried the century, while trumpeters blew into the slender tin bodies of their instruments as though their lives depended on it. But perhaps deep in their musical hearts, they knew that the next century would not regard the trumpet with such favor.

JOSEPH HAYDN AND HIS VALVE

We know already that the Aida trumpet was invented by Giuseppe Verdi. In the 18th century, the celebrated composer Joseph Haydn tried to enliven one of his concertos with the sound of a trumpet in which holes had been drilled. But the sound of the tin tubes of the time certainly wasn't improved by this innovation. The time had come for valved trumpets, which we still use today.

OLDEST WORKING TRUMPETS

The two oldest working trumpets originate from around 1260 BCE. One of these military bugles is made of copper, the other of silver. They were discovered by archaeologists in 1922, in the tomb of the pharaoh Tutankhamun. It is said that this tomb is cursed, and superstition also attaches to the trumpets. On the very day scientists tried to coax a sound from the silver bugle, it is said that the electricity supply for the whole of Egypt was cut. Coincidence or not? What do you think?

I drill a small hole there and we will see.

FAMOUS TRUMPET PLAYERS

DIZZY GILLESPIE

BENT TRUMPET

LOUIS ARMSTRONG

Louis Armstrong (1900–1971), one of the most brilliant jazz trumpeters of the 20th century, took up the trumpet while in a house of correction for children. He had a clear aim: to become a professional musician. By the 1930s, he was indeed a musician, and a famous one too. In Europe, he played for the British king; later, he would be given his own star on the Hollywood Walk of Fame. All it took was courage, talent, and a lot of hard work.

My child's dream? To be a famous trumpeter.

LOUIS ARMSTRONG

DIZZY GILLESPIE

Have you ever heard of a trumpeter who is happy to play a bent horn? Well, Dizzy Gillespie (1917–1993) was one such. A true virtuoso of the trumpet and a remarkable on-stage showman, he was involved in an accident in which his instrument was damaged. But Dizzy was so delighted by the distorted sound of the damaged instrument that he came to prefer it to any other.

COMPOSERS

JOSEPH HAYDN

JOHANN SEBASTIAN BACH

On his journey through the world of musical instruments, Niccolo heard the name of the great Johann Sebastian Bach (1685–1750) several times. Now he was hearing it in connection with the trumpet. For this instrument, Bach composed *Brandenburg Concerto No. 2 in F major*, one of the most important compositions of the Baroque period and one of the hardest works for a trumpeter to play.

JOHANN SEBASTIAN BACH

JOSEPH HAYDN

The works of Austrian composer Joseph Haydn (1732–1809) include his *Trumpet Concerto in E-flat major*, which he wrote when his reputation was already high. It is the earliest such work in which the trumpet is the solo instrument, and it was perhaps made possible by Haydn's great fame. Until then, the trumpet's role had been very limited.

MILITARY BAND

Music was an accompaniment to armed conflict from prehistoric times. It encouraged the warriors, set a rhythm, and gave emphasis to commands. The louder the instruments played, the better. No wonder, then, that military music spilled over into the formation of bands with many members playing woodwind, brass, and percussion instruments.

TROMBONE

BASS FLUGELHORN

CLARINET

TRUMPET

FLUTE

CYMBALS

BIG DRUM

SNARE DRUM

BASS HORN

BASSOON

RELATIVES OF THE TRUMPET
WIND INSTRUMENTS

"All these different trumpets are making me confused," said Niccolo, as he continued his musical pilgrimage. "But what's this?" At his next stop, there are lots more metal objects. Welcome to the world of Miss Trumpet's cousins! These instruments include saxophones, trombones, sousaphones, and helicons. Trum-ta-ta-daa! Too-too-oo!

FLUGELHORN

At first sight, you might confuse it with a trumpet, but when you look closer, you realize that the flugelhorn is a little larger, has a wider tube, and is more cone-shaped at the end. All this makes its sound softer, fuller, and less sharp than that of the trumpet, its slenderer sister—as we hear clearly in wind orchestras.

CORNET

Something between a flugelhorn and a trumpet, this instrument has its origins in the posthorn. Although its tone is not as full as the trumpet's, at one time it threatened the latter's existence, as it is more comfortable to play. In appearance, it is like a pocket-sized trumpet.

FUGELHORN

TUBA

Playing the tuba requires a lot of strength, so the player must be sitting comfortably to bear its weight. Its deep, bass sound is heard in orchestras accompanying other instruments.

TROMBONE

This instrument has quite a long history. Indeed, having been played since the 15th century, it is one of the oldest metal instruments. The slide trombone is composed of two parts. The trombone's tone is changed by moving the slide up and down. There is also a valve trombone, which is somewhat easier to play—to extend the instrument to the required length, the player just presses down on a valve.

TROMBONE

TUBA

BENT TUBE

SOUSAPHONE

SOUSAPHONE

A brother of the helicon, this instrument was named after John Philip Sousa, an American composer and conductor, and is popular with American military bands for its bolder, sharper sound. And its bent tube means that it fits around the player's body, allowing them to march proudly as they blow.

FRENCH HORN

This bent brass instrument is known for its lovely velvety tone. Having started out as a military instrument, it was also used for the playing of fanfares and to give signals at the hunts. Although it is made of metal, its shape continues to resemble a cow horn, out of which it developed. Today, the French horn has been promoted from the hunt to the symphony orchestra and chamber ensemble. Its long tones are also heard in jazz music.

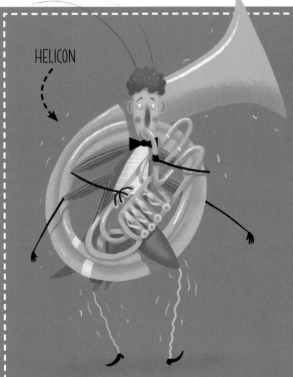

HELICON

HELICON

A helicon is a kind of tuba modified so that the player can bear its weight comfortably on the shoulder without the need to sit. Indeed, helicon players can march briskly as they blow their horns. In the Balkans, the helicon is a much-loved instrument and, as such, an inseparable part of the folk tradition.

HUNTING HORN

I bet the hunt is starting!

ADOLPHE SAX

"When I grow up, I'd like to invent and build an instrument that will go down in the history of music," the Belgian Adolphe Sax (1814–1894) would say to himself in his younger years. He practiced hard to be ready to enjoy his success. When he was only six years old, he started work on a clarinet. "What should my new instrument be like?" he wondered. "Easy to handle, like a woodwind instrument, but with a rich sound, like a brass one." Which is precisely what he made. The public first heard the new saxophone in 1841. It combined the fingering of the wooden oboe with the solid sound of metal. Where did the name come from? It was named after the inventor Sax, of course!

WHAT A BIG SOUND!

The saxophone didn't really catch on for the playing of the classics: it was simply too loud to play the gentle melodies of world-famous compositions. But where a powerful sound was needed, it truly shone. In the late 1840s, there was a competition for military bands in France. Just guess which orchestra was the clear winner! That's right, the one with the saxophones, which outplayed all the others. After that, Adolphe Sax was commissioned to equip all French military bands with his saxophones.

SAXOPHONES

As with many other instruments, there are different kinds of saxophones, ordered by size. Take a look!

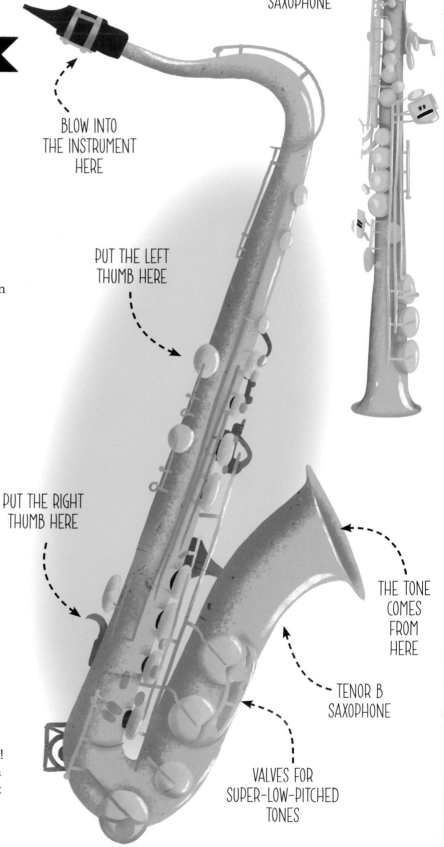

SOPRANO E SAXOPHONE

BLOW INTO THE INSTRUMENT HERE

PUT THE LEFT THUMB HERE

PUT THE RIGHT THUMB HERE

THE TONE COMES FROM HERE

TENOR B SAXOPHONE

VALVES FOR SUPER-LOW-PITCHED TONES

GOLDEN AGE OF THE SAXOPHONE

In the early 20th century, a new type of music called jazz began to spread across America. The saxophone was as well suited to jazz as it had been to the military band, and it was taken up by many jazz musicians. The popularity of Adolphe Sax's beautiful instruments grew as jazz blossomed all over the world.

ALTHOUGH THE **SAXOPHONE** IS MADE OF METAL, IT IS NOT A BRASS INSTRUMENT. **BECAUSE OF ITS CONSTRUCTION,** IT IS CONSIDERED **A WOODWIND INSTRUMENT.**

CHARLIE PARKER

CONTRABASS SAXOPHONE

CHARLIE PARKER

Before he became a famous saxophonist, Charlie Parker (1920–1955) made a poor living in glamorous New York washing dishes. When he had time in the evening, he would meet up with fellow musicians for a jam. It wasn't long before fate and his incredible talent took him from the dirty pots and pans to the musical heavens. In the 1940s, Parker became one of the best jazzmen in New York. His glory was short-lived, however—Parker's lifestyle and a lack of acceptance for his music beyond the city brought this brilliant horn player to his knees.

ANGELA DAVIS

ANGELA DAVIS

Angela Davis, who was born in Australia in 1985, was so good in her field that she earned a Masters of Music degree in it. Now she appears alongside the very best at the most prestigious jazz festivals.

PRACTICE MAKES PERFECT!

If you want to be a phenomenal saxophonist you must practice very hard. And the sooner your start, the better. Niccolo should grab his shiny saxophone right now and start blowing into it with all his strength every day from morning to evening!

DIXIELAND JAZZ

Unlike a big band, a Dixieland band plays improvised jazz. It is based around a trombone, a trumpet, a saxophone, and a clarinet, supplemented with a rhythm section comprising a piano and drums. Some later Dixieland bands added a sousaphone and replaced the piano with a guitar or a banjo.

DOUBLE BASS

SAXOPHONE

TROMBONE

CLARINET

J.C. DIXI BAND

DRUMS

PIANO

Jenny's

41

FLUTES & WOODWIND INSTRUMENTS
WIND INSTRUMENTS

REED

"What's that whistling sound?" wondered Niccolo. He and Luciano hurried off to find out. They found a skinny little boy sitting on the floor, blowing into a wooden flute with all his might, his fingers racing up and down its holes. The twisting melody rose above him in pleasing shapes. Niccolo thought it fantastic.

PAN

INSTRUMENT OF THE GODS

According to the ancient Egyptians, the flute was the invention of Osiris, god of the afterlife and rebirth, and one of their most powerful gods. As a result, the flute was treated with great respect in Egypt. An end-blown flute called a men was held perpendicular to the mouth (like today's recorder). The sebi flute was played rather like today's transverse (side-blown) flute.

MOUTHPIECE

HEAD

INTRODUCING THE RECORDER

The flute known as the recorder is a wind instrument made of wood or plastic. It has a thumb hole and seven finger holes. The first recorders were made from a single piece of wood. Today's recorders are made from three parts—head, body, and foot. The player holds the recorder more or less perpendicular to the mouth, blows into the mouthpiece at one end, and covers or uncovers the finger holes with the fingers. This covering and uncovering of the holes allows different notes to sound.

BODY

PAN FLUTE (SYRINX)

The ancient Greeks attributed the flute with a divine origin. The god Pan played multiple single-note pipes of gradually increasing length. These pipes were made of reed, cane, bamboo, or wood. But time has moved on and demanded modernization—these days, pan flutes of plastic, metal, or glass are not unusual.

FOOT

RECORDER

TYPES OF RECORDER

There are many kinds of recorder. The smallest, called the piccolo (or garklein), is half the size of the standard instrument. Piccolos, too, are made of wood or metal. Those with a liking for lower notes prefer the alto or the bass recorder, although these instruments are played less often.

! FOR AN **ASPIRING MUSICIAN** WHO WANTS TO PLAY **A WIND INSTRUMENT,** THE RECORDER IS THE BEST PLACE TO START.

SOPRANINO • SOPRANO • ALTO • TENOR • BASS • DOUBLE BASS

CHOOSE THE ONE YOU WANT

Niccolo was puzzled by all the recorders on offer. Which one should he choose? How about one of the smaller ones? If so, should he try the sopranino or the piccolo, whose notes are higher than sopranino's? After the high-tuned soprano come the mellifluous alto, the tenor, the bass, and the 6-foot-long double bass ... Niccolo was in a quandary. It was a tough nut to crack—could Luciano help him?

ICE AGE

Whistles and flutes—of all sizes, vertical, and transverse—are among the oldest musical instruments in the world. Archaeological finds have proven that flute playing goes all the way back to the Stone Age. Early flautists entertained others on pipes made of bamboo, wood, or bone. One of the world's oldest flutes—made of reindeer bone 22,000 years ago—was found in the Pyrenees; it has just one hole, so it can produce only one note.

TRANSVERSE FLUTE

Toot your flute!

TRANSVERSE (SIDE-BLOWN) FLUTE

Like the recorder, the transverse flute is considered a woodwind instrument, even though most such flutes are made exclusively of metal. As its name suggests, this flute is held horizontal from the mouth. It is such an important instrument that we find it in symphony orchestras, brass bands, and chamber ensembles. Unlike the recorder, which has open holes in the body, the transverse flute boasts keys above the holes and key axles, which close the keys automatically.

43

MEDIEVAL FLUTES AND PIPES

Although the music of the pious Middle Ages prioritized the human voice, people continued to enjoy instrumental music. Wandering conjurers would play flutes in town streets. In rural areas, meanwhile, flutes and pipes became important instruments of folk music.

RENAISSANCE

In the Renaissance period, music emerged from the churches and cathedrals and was found more and more often in the streets. Two holes for the little finger were added to the recorder. One of these holes was covered over with wax, depending on the hand the player used for the instrument. Until the late 16th century, when the first flutes made of two pieces of wood were made, the recorder comprised just a single piece. During the Renaissance, the flute became popular all over Europe.

OFF YOU GO, DEAR RECORDER

The recorder did not enjoy the limelight for long. In the second half of the 18th century, its popularity faded, and its place was taken by the transverse flute. The main reason for this change was the demand for instruments with an intense, powerful sound, something the recorder could not achieve. But folk music did not renounce the recorder, which explains how it has survived to the present day.

GOLDEN AGE OF THE FLUTE

The Baroque period was the golden age of the flute. It became so popular with musicians that they often chose it as a solo instrument. At that time, the flute became composed of three parts, making it very similar to today's instrument. The floodgates opened on the use of the recorder as a solo concert instrument. Bach, Vivaldi, and Handel wrote music especially for it.

JOHANN JOACHIM QUANTZ

JOHANN JOACHIM QUANTZ

"Remember this man's name, Niccolo," Luciano whispered into the cricket's ear. Born at the end of the 18th century in Germany, Johann Joachim Quantz (1697–1773) devoted his life to the flute. He has gone down in history as an outstanding flautist and composer. Most of the music he wrote was for the flute. Plus, to get others to love the transverse flute as much as he did, Joachim wrote *On Playing the Flute*, a treatise on flute performance, in which he drew from his vast experience as a virtuoso of this instrument.

JEAN-PIERRE RAMPAL

This Frenchman worked hard his whole life to get people to accept the transverse flute as a solo concert instrument. In addition, he taught many outstanding flautists at the Conservatoire de Paris. Jean-Pierre Rampal was born in 1922 and died in 2000.

JEAN-PIERRE RAMPAL

IAN ANDERSON

"Anyone who tells me the flute isn't modern can get stuffed!" said Niccolo angrily. With good reason. Think of the legendary rock band Jethro Tull. Their frontman Ian Anderson (born 1947) is a brilliant flute player, and, believe it or not, the transverse flute and rock music are a perfect match. As well as the transverse flute, Anderson plays many other flutes and pipes.

IAN ANDERSON

SOME PREFERRED THE OBOE ...

STAPLE

The oboe, too, is one of the world's oldest instruments. Indeed, its sound was enjoyed in the 12th century BCE by people in China and India. Originally, this beautiful instrument had no holes—the sound was produced by the vibration of air between two reeds. The oboe was very popular in the Arab world, where 22 oboe-type instruments were produced. Having arrived in Europe in the 18th century, it was immediately prized for its beautiful tone.

OBOE

GEORG FRIEDRICH HANDEL

This famous German-born composer of the 17th and 18th centuries studied law before turning to music—specifically the organ, harpsichord, and violin. He so enjoyed the gentle, melancholy tones of the oboe that he composed several sonatas for oboe. Later when he wrote music for an orchestra, he liked to include important passages for the oboe. And why not? Georg Friedrich Handel (1685–1759) could play many instruments, and he was an excellent oboist.

KEYS MECHANISM

HAVE YOU GOT ENOUGH AIR?

Playing the oboe isn't easy. In fact, it can be pretty exhausting. An oboist fills his lungs with air before releasing it into his instrument very slowly. It may not appear so, but this technique causes blood to flow to the head very quickly. For this reason, during concerts, oboists need to take lots of breaks; if they didn't, they might faint.

GEORG FRIEDRICH HANDEL

BELL

- - COR ANGLAIS

COR ANGLAIS

The cor anglais is a double-reed woodwind instrument of the oboe family. It is used in symphony orchestras in particular. The cor anglais is longer than the oboe, and its sound is a perfect fifth lower. Unlike the oboe, it ends in a pear-shaped bell, which gives it a warm, mellow sound. As the fingering is very similar to that of the oboe, it is easy for an oboist to play the cor anglais. Amusingly, this instrument has nothing to do with England, as its name suggests. The name comes from the curved shape of the instrument that today's cor anglais originated from, which in French was nicknamed "cor anglé," meaning "curved horn." Over time this was corrupted to "cor anglais" ("English horn").

SHAWM

An ancestor of the oboe and the cor anglais, this double-reed woodwind instrument reached Europe from the Arab world at the time of the Crusades. In many countries, it has survived in various forms to the present day. It is widely used in traditional folk music, especially in the Mediterranean region, the Balkans, Spain, and Portugal.

- - SHAWM

BELL RING

BASSOON

Do you want to play something sorrowful? Enter the bassoon, a wooden bass instrument with its origins in 17th-century Italy. As this instrument is 8 feet tall, its sounding tube is in two parts, which are tied together. It is from this that its Italian name fagotto— meaning "bundle of sticks"— derives. The bassoon is a very versatile instrument—as well as sounding sorrowful, it can sound merry, amorous, and tender.

BASSOON

BOCAL (CROOK)

BASS JOINT

STRAP RING

PROTECTOR CAP

IT'S CRUCIAL TO GET THE RIGHT EMBOUCHURE

To play a wind instrument properly, getting the embouchure right is crucial. This means dropping the jaw and engaging and arranging the facial muscles in the appropriate way for the instrument you are playing. The embouchure affects the intonation of your playing and the quality of the note. Whoever wishes to play a wind instrument must work hard on their embouchure.

W. A. MOZART

Wind instruments surely appealed to the musical ears of Wolfgang Amadeus Mozart (1756–1791), the most famous composer of all time. After his stays in Mannheim and Paris, he came to love the sound of the clarinet in particular. At that time, it was a new instrument, and Wolfi was captivated by it. So inspired was he by its sound that he composed separate concertos for French horn, clarinet, bassoon, oboe, and flute, although he was not very fond of the latter.

CARNEGIE HALL, ON NEW YORK'S SEVENTH AVENUE, IS **THE WORLD'S MOST PRESTIGIOUS VENUE** FOR THE PERFORMANCE OF **CLASSICAL AND POPULAR MUSIC.**

BENNY GOODMAN

CLARINET

MOUTHPIECE

BARREL

CLARINET

The clarinet is descended from an ancient instrument with a poetic name. The shawm came to Europe from the Arab world with the Crusades. The clarinet as we know it originated around 1720. It is called "clarinet" because its higher sounds are reminiscent of the trumpet (clarino). The clarinet joined the orchestra in the second half of the 18th century (the period of Neoclassicism). As tends to happen, the clarinet was a forerunner of other instruments—the saxophone, for instance.

BELL

BENNY GOODMAN

"Your cricket's brain should remember this name, Niccolo." Benny Goodman, known as the "King of Swing," was a legendary American swing and jazz musician who lived from 1909 to 1986. He was such an outstanding clarinettist that his jazz band appeared at the famous Carnegie Hall in 1938.

WOODY ALLEN

WOODY ALLEN

The sound of the clarinet and jazz also holds US film director, dramatist, and writer Woody Allen (real name Allan Stewart Könisgberg) in its thrall. Born in 1935, he learned to play the clarinet as a child. He was so captivated by the instrument that it inspired him in his choice of pseudonym, which celebrates the famous clarinettist Woody Herman. Clarinet playing is more than just a hobby for four-time Oscar winner Allen: he appears regularly with the New Orleans Jazz Band and has even undertaken a large European tour with the band.

ROCK BAND

A rock band is a group of musicians who play rock music. In the 1980s and 1990s, rock bands played to sell-out crowds in stadiums. No rock band worth its salt can be without an electric guitar, a bass guitar, drums, and keyboards, including a Hammond organ and synthesizers.

BASS GUITAR

DRUM SET

ELECTRIC
GUITAR

HAMMOND
ORGAN

GUITAR & LUTE
PLUCKED INSTRUMENTS

PLUCKED

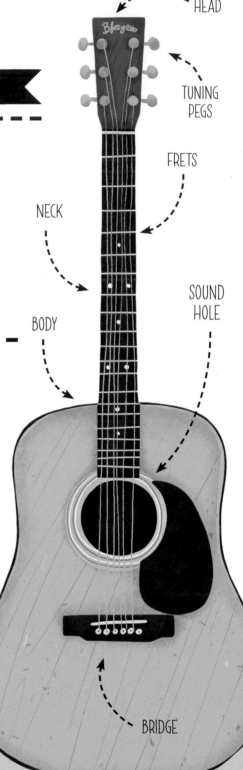

HEAD

TUNING PEGS

FRETS

NECK

SOUND HOLE

BODY

BRIDGE

Strummed and plucked notes from a guitar could be heard all along the street. Eyes closed, brow puckered, and fingers racing up and down the fretboard, this guy was playing as if his life depended on it. As one chord followed another, the catchy melody pleased the musical ears of six-legged Niccolo and two-legged Luciano. "I couldn't do without the guitar," said Niccolo, as he danced to the rhythm and set out in search of another instrument.

WHAT IS A GUITAR?

A guitar is a stringed instrument for plucking and strumming. These days, most guitars have six strings. The guitar produces notes and chords on the principle of resonance, like a piano. The strings are played with the fingernails or a plectrum so that they vibrate and achieve the desired sound. The vibration characteristics depend on the material of the body of the guitar.

PARTS OF A GUITAR

HEAD
This is the place where the strings are attached to the tuning pegs.

TUNING PEGS
This is used for tuning the strings. Turning a peg either loosens or tightens the string, thus giving it a lower or higher note

NECK
The fretboard forms part of the neck; the frets form the fretboard.

FRETS
These are metal strips, which divide the fretboard into semitone intervals.

BODY
This basic part determines the sound of the guitar.

BRIDGE
This holds the strings fast to the instrument.

SOUND HOLE
This is in the very center of the guitar.

THE VERY OLDEST

Like the piano, the guitar has developed into what it is today over many years. In quest of its origins, Niccolo and Luciano went all the way back to ancient times and found themselves in Western Asia in 2500 BCE. On a clay tablet, an artist from the Sumerian city of Nippur produced an image of a musician playing an instrument that looks like a square guitar. Called a kinnor, it is one of the very first plucked instruments and is mentioned in the Bible.

KINNOR

HITTITE GUITAR

A step closer to the guitar we know today, this long-necked, fretted instrument had a flat body and many sound holes. It was a favorite instrument of the Hittites, an ancient people from Asia Minor. Around 1600 BCE, the Hittites invaded Egypt, and soon their stringed instrument became popular in the mighty empire by the Nile; it was known as the Egyptian lute.

Such a pity no one can hear me . . .

HITTITE GUITAR

MUSIC ON THREE STRINGS

The ancient Greeks enjoyed playing a stringed instrument called a cithara. Although this word is very like the modern "guitar," the two instruments are rather different. The cithara of the ancients was more like a lyre than a guitar.

ROMANCE IN THE MIDDLE AGES

Thank goodness for those valiant, chivalrous medieval heroes known as knights! A knight would delight the lady of his heart with a song of love. And if his pleasing voice was accompanied by the melody of quavering strings, the lady might even fall at his feet. In the 12th century, the popularity of the guitar spread to many corners of the world along with troubadours, Minnesänger, and bards.

THE LATIN GUITAR AT LAST

All these stringed forefathers and -mothers took inspiration from each other. The next few centuries saw the emergence of the beautiful guitarra latina (Latin guitar), whose figure-eight shape made it very like the guitar of today. It was used for accompanying singers and as a solo instrument.

CITHARA

LUTE

"LUTE" WAS USED UNTIL THE 15TH CENTURY AS A GENERAL TERM FOR **A WIDE RANGE OF STRINGED,** PLUCKED INSTRUMENTS.

BASIC GUITAR TYPES

CLASSICAL (SPANISH)

This is the oldest type in use, usually for the playing of classical music. These days, it is also used in the playing of jazz, country, folk, and popular music.

CLASSICAL GUITAR

ACOUSTIC

ACOUSTIC GUITAR

This has a narrower fretboard and more powerful sound than the classical guitar. Basically, it is used in all genres of music—pop, rock, jazz, swing, country, folk, you name it!

HAWAIIAN

You won't find metal frets on its fretboard, which is smooth.

SEMI-ACOUSTIC GUITAR

HAWAIIAN GUITAR

SEMI-ACOUSTIC

This is a special guitar with pick-ups and a hollow body with F-shaped sound holes, like a violin.

ELECTRIC

As it does not have a hollow body, the sound of the strings is read by a pick-up connected to an amplifier. A staple in heavy metal, rock, and rock 'n' roll, the electric guitar has real zest.

ELECTRIC GUITAR

SPAIN AND THE GUITAR

Although Spain is not the birthplace of the guitar, it is in this land on the Iberian Peninsula that its thousand-year evolution reached its zenith. Spain was first the home of an instrument called the vihuela, played with the fingers, a plectrum, or a bow. In Italy, the vihuela was known as the viola. And because the guitar and its like are often connected with merrymaking, it was described as the instrument of Italian commedia dell'arte performers.

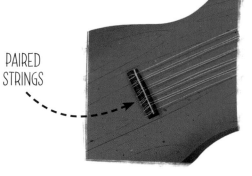

SPANISH GUITAR

FOUR, FIVE, OR SIX?

Vihuelas had doubled strings known as paired courses. While the Renaissance was partial to four paired courses, the Baroque period preferred five. From the second half of the 18th century, six paired courses became popular.

PAIRED STRINGS

ARE WE COOL?

What's more, in the 18th century, the guitar became very fashionable. Young people liked to play it, men and women alike. As happens with fashions, the guitar would later lose its popularity for a while, although in good old Spain it would remain as popular as ever. "All these guitars are making my head spin. What on earth can we call an 'ordinary guitar?' One thing's for sure, though—I must have a guitar in my little orchestra! I'll get myself one and start practicing really hard. I'd love to play like . . ."

FERNANDO SOR

FERNANDO SOR

Fernando Sor (1778–1839) was a Spanish composer and guitarist. He was considered the Beethoven of the guitar. Study of his works—of which there are over sixty—is today indispensable in the basic education of young, classical guitar beginners.

MAURO GIULIANI

Mauro Giuliani (1781–1829) was another composer and guitarist of the same era, this time from Italy. He went on a grand tour, delighting concert goers all over Europe with his virtuoso playing. Not for nothing was he invited into Austrian aristocratic circles; not for nothing did he appear and work alongside Ludwig van Beethoven at important concerts in Vienna.

MAURO GIULIANI

ANDRÉS SEGOVIA

ANDRÉS SEGOVIA

Spain's Andrés Segovia (1893–1987) was one of the most phenomenal guitarists of the 20th century. He was a pioneer in bringing the guitar to concert halls. By his amazing playing, he demonstrated the full distinctive sound of the guitar and its technical potential. Before Segovia, the guitar was considered an instrument that greatly improved the atmosphere in cafés. It is amazing to think that Andrés Segovia's brilliant guitar playing was achieved without a teacher, through his own hard work, talent, and intuition. He was still playing concerts in his nineties.

JIMI HENDRIX

Let us return to the more recent past—to the America of the second half of the 20th century. The hugely talented Jimi Hendrix (1942–1970) used his guitar to write rock history. He knew nothing of musical notation or music theory, yet he played like a god. From the age of fifteen, he forever had first a battered Spanish guitar and then a very cheap electric guitar in his hands. He learned to play by listening to records played on the radio. Although a left-hander, he played an instrument strung for right-handers. He was only 27 when he died, but his immortal guitar solos will always gladden the hearts of lovers of rock music.

JIMI HENDRIX

STRUGGLING NICCOLO

MORE ABOUT JIMI

Just imagine, children—not only has Niccolo the cricket played a guitar that once belonged to John Lennon, one of the famous Beatles; he has even clawed at the strings of Jimi Hendrix's instrument. He was so inspired by the experience that he spent the rest of that day trying to get his fingers around the chords. What about Luciano? He sang his heart out until the sun went down.

ALL THAT IS PLUCKED & STRUMMED

The guitar isn't the only instrument that is plucked and strummed, of course. Niccolo the cricket finds himself in the string kingdom. Strings metal and nylon; strings tighter and looser; strings in and out of tune. As you can see for yourself, the guitar isn't the only musical instrument to be plucked and strummed.

LUTE

Like the guitar, the lute is one of the most important of all instruments. Its roots reach all the way back to ancient Mesopotamia—i.e., 4,000 years. The first lute was probably made from a hollowed-out pumpkin with an animal skin pulled over it, to which was attached a wooden neck. The lute arrived in Europe from the Arab lands through good old Spain, which has strumming and plucking in its blood.

LUTE

THE LUTE AND FAMOUS COMPOSERS

Johann Sebastian Bach, one of the greatest composers of the 17th and 18th centuries, wrote music for the lute, too. The works of Joseph Haydn, another musical colossus of the 18th century, include compositions for the lute and stringed instruments.

BANJO

The banjo is the baby of the family of stringed instruments. The first banjo was made in 1831 by an American musician called Joel Walker Sweeney. He was inspired by an instrument played by slaves, which they taught Sweeney to play when he was a boy. He simply exchanged the gourd body for a wooden one and added an extra string to the slaves' four. Sweeney took his banjo all over America. Believe it or not, by the standards of the day, he was a real star.

BANJO

JACQUES GAULTIER

Frenchman Jacques Gaultier (1617–1652) was an outstanding virtuoso of the lute in the 17th century. On his concert tours, Gaultier discovered and made popular the so-called Maler lute, named after a luthier from Bologna called Laux Maler.

AN OLD LADY?

The harp can be proud of its longevity. If it had the power of memory, it would remember Mesopotamia and ancient Egypt. Can you guess what came before the harp? That's right—an ordinary bow. We have the bow to thank for giving us the idea for the harp. When the bowstring was pulled to release the arrow, the bowstring "played" a lovely pluck. People wondered what this sound would be like if it was louder and there were more such sounds. With the creation of the harp, they found out.

HARP

"Phew! This is way too heavy for me! Lifting a harp like this is an inhuman task. This concert instrument weighs 80 pounds, and it is almost 6 feet tall and almost 4 feet long. If you do manage to lift it, try playing it and not getting caught up in its 47 strings! It's anything but child's play, I can tell you." Look at poor Niccolo!

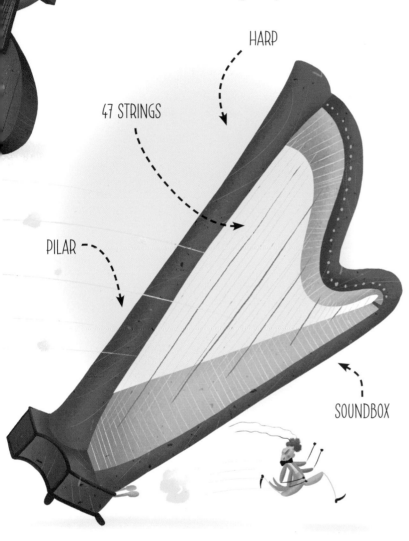

HARP

47 STRINGS

PILAR

SOUNDBOX

TO LOCK OR TO UNLOCK?

A proper harp must be properly tuned—using a key not dissimilar to those used to wind old clocks. But make sure you don't turn the key too briskly. If you do, you'll break a string or two. A missing little finger is no obstacle to playing the harp—the harp is played with the ball of the thumb and the tips of the index finger, middle finger, and ring finger.

HURDY-GURDY

This is making my head spin, said Niccolo in amazement. Luciano twisted and twisted to the sound until he was wound up in his own neck. The vibration of the six strings of the hurdy-gurdy is achieved by turning a key on the strange instrument's side. In case you're thinking that the hurdy-gurdy is an instrument of no consequence, let me tell you that Mozart, Vivaldi, and Chopin all composed for it.

Get the handle right.

PIPHAT

A piphat is a medium-sized ensemble playing local classical music to accompany performances of traditional Thai theater and dance. The main instruments are woodwind, xylophone, and drums. It is said that piphat music represents the dance of Thai dragons.

THE GONG CIRCLE

XYLOPHONE

OBOE

XYLOPHONE

DRUMS

INDIRECT TREMBLING

TREMBLING

And so our two friends wandered on, searching and finding. Many unusual folk and ethnic instruments crossed their path, some better known than others. Some they blew into, some they strummed or plucked, while others they just gazed at in awe.

BEAUTY IN SIMPLICITY

Don't look for any complexity in the didgeridoo. The first didgeridoo was just a eucalyptus log gnawed hollow by termites, which Aborigines had cleaned carefully and to which they added a mouthpiece of wild beeswax on its narrower side. All they needed to do then was put it to the lips and blow—thus producing the didgeridoo's unmistakeable, long-drawn-out tone.

! IN AUSTRALIA, WALL PAINTINGS DEPICTING **THE DIDGERIDOO SURVIVE** FROM **PREHISTORIC TIMES.**

DIDGERIDOO

Niccolo and Luciano found the strangely named didgeridoo in Australia, where it comes from. Native Australians, known as Aborigines, have played the didgeridoo for so long that no one can say when they started. Perhaps this long, hollow tube, originally made of hard eucalyptus wood, is as much as 40,000 years old, making it the proud owner of the title World's Oldest Musical Instrument.

THE FIRST DIDGERIDOO

Once upon a time, there was an Aborigine who went into the forest for wood. As he was gathering the wood, he found a eucalyptus log filled with termites, which had hollowed it out with their mandibles. Not wanting to burn the termites in the fire, the man blew into the log to drive them out and save them. As he was blowing, the log produced a tone of incredible beauty. "What a shame it would be to burn this wood!" the Aborigine said to himself and thus the didgeridoo was born.

He-e-elp! That man has blown us out!

THE CELESTIAL SOUND OF CHINA

"Where are those bittersweet tones coming from?" asked Niccolo, as he walked towards the plaintive song, as if in a daze. "So tender, so caressing, so melancholy . . . The wind carries them through the land, drapes them over the treetops, and puts them in the hearts of lonely people. Where do they come from, and who is making them?" "Welcome to the magical world of a Chinese folk instrument called the erhu," whispered Luciano, as he pointed with his beak at the girl musician.

SOME ERHU PLAYERS CAN COAX FROM THEIR INSTRUMENT SOUNDS OF NATURE, **SUCH AS THE WARBLING OF BIRDS**, RAINFALL HEAVY AND LIGHT, A STORM, OR **A FAST-FLOWING RIVER.**

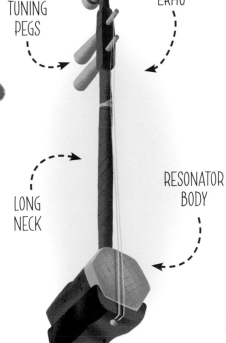

TUNING PEGS

ERHU

LONG NECK

RESONATOR BODY

A PEERLESS TRADITION

A charming Chinese instrument called the erhu can draw on a thousand-year tradition. The erhu is an integral part of all Chinese folk festivals, theater performances, operas, and gala imperial events.

SYMBOLISM OF THE CELESTIAL LUTE

The celestial lute, which at first glance looks rather like a pear, is three feet and five inches long with good reason. The number three represents the heavens, Earth, and man, while five refers to the five elements—fire, water, wood, earth, and metal. The pipa's four strings represent the seasons of the year.

LONG LIVE THE KING!

It is no exaggeration to say that the beautiful pipa is the true king of Chinese folk musical instruments. Immortalized in the wall paintings of the Mogao Caves near Dunhuang, it has been played for many centuries. You could be forgiven for thinking the tones of the pipa were music from the heavens.

PIPA PLAYER

PIPA

JAPANESE MUSICAL INSTRUMENTS

It's not far from China to Japan. A stretch by air, a stretch by train, and our two friends find themselves in the Land of the Rising Sun. Before they know it, they are admiring the oriental tones of a trio of local instruments—a flute called the shakuhachi, a stringed instrument called the shamisen, and a zither known as the koto.

MONK PLAYING SHAKUHACHI

IN THE BEGINNING WERE THE MONKS

Before the bamboo flute known as the shakuhachi became a concert instrument, it served monks of the Japanese Fuke sect as an important aid in a breathing exercise. These impoverished holy men sometimes needed to earn a little extra to feed themselves, which they did by playing the shakuhachi. In this way, people got to know this unremarkable-looking flute.

SHAKUHACHI BAMBOO FLUTE

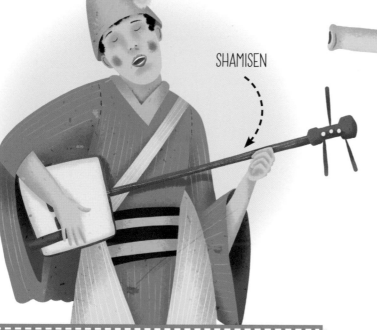

SHAMISEN

KOTO

While the shamisen has three strings, the koto has thirteen! Like the shamisen, the koto is derived from a Chinese instrument—the five-stringed guzheng, which arrived in Japan in the 7th century. Almost 6 feet long, the koto is made from kiri wood and its plectrums from ivory. The player needs an excellent musical ear, as it is hard to keep the sensitive koto in tune.

SHAMISEN

The gentle tones of the shamisen are often played by the delicate fingers of a white-faced geisha. Musicians use a plectrum to pluck the three strings of this long-necked Japanese flute as they accompany the traditional Japanese theater known as kabuki. The origins of the shamisen are found in the Chinese sanxian, which reached the islands of Japan in the 16th century. It was then adapted and modified by local musicians for their own uses.

THE TRADITIONAL KOTO HAS 13 STRINGS; SOME KOTOS HAVE 20.

AFRICA & DRUMS

Boom, boom, boom. Boom-ta-ra-taa, boom, boom, boom. Scorched by the golden sun, the African continent speaks in drumbeats. Niccolo and Luciano know some drums already, but others are found only here, in the warm heart of Africa.

! THE DJEMBE IS NOT USED IN RITUALS. **IT WAS FIRST MANUFACTURED** BY ORDINARY SMITHS, WHO PLAYED IT TO PASS THE TIME WHILE **THEY WERE SMELTING IRON.**

DJEMBE

The djembe drum is shaped like a chalice or an African pot in which women pulverize millet. The locals make it from a single piece of African mahogany, hollowing out a tree trunk with their hands—just imagine! The sound of the djembe depends on the quality of its interior.

DJEMBE

ORIGINS OF THE DJEMBE

According to legend, one day in a forest, a hunter called So Dyeu met a chimpanzee merrily beating a djembe. The sound of the drum so charmed the young man that he decided to make it his. He dug a hole in the ground, set a trap, and waited for the monkey to be caught in it. The next day, he found the ape drummer cowering at the bottom of the pit. The hunter took the drum and returned with his prize to the village. It is said that the sound of the djembe are voices of the souls of dead chimpanzee drummers.

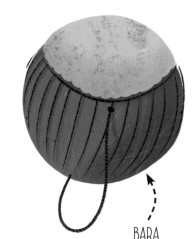

BARA

SICO

BARA DRUM

Africans are very fond of drums. No public holiday would be complete without a spherical hand drum known as a bara. This drum's special shape comes from the fact that it is made from a dried gourd, part of which is cut off to be replaced with the goatskin head. Bara drums come in various sizes.

A SQUARE DRUM

Have you never seen a square drum? Well, they have one in Africa. Called a sico, it comprises a wooden frame with a goatskin head. The sico is commonly played in a group of five musicians, with each drum making a different sound. The five drums each have their own name—wamban, baba, solo, rolling, and toublok.

INDIA

It would be unthinkable to exclude India from a quest for musical instruments—and Luciano would never forgive Niccolo if he did! The melodies made by Indian instruments express the purity of deities. Indians still believe that musical instruments are the work of the gods. Hear for yourself.

PUNGI

EKTARA

The very oldest Indian musical instrument, the ektara is a great example of beauty in simplicity. It is nothing but an ordinary gourd through which is inserted a stick of bamboo with a single string along its length. It's a musical wonder!

EKTARA

WAKING A SNAKE

Any visitor to India must try out a pungi, the instrument of the Indian snake charmer. It consists of a small gourd with two pipes and a hole to blow into. Its sharp, penetrating sound is the work of two reeds in the pipes. Although the pungi is a small, unremarkable-looking instrument, its sound is so strong that it can wake the sleepiest snake.

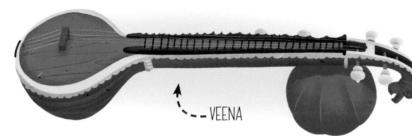

VEENA

VEENA

The veena is an instrument created by the god Shiva, with a tone that resembles the human voice. It is best suited to spiritual music. Most veena players are women. The veena has four main strings and three extra strings that play the lower notes.

GHATAM

GHATAM

"It isn't a water jug, honestly!" laughed Luciano, as the confused Niccolo turned the strange clay pot around in his cricket mits. "It's called a ghatam." When struck with the fingers, palms, thumbs, or nails (each of which produces a different sound), this percussion instrument truly sings. "If you want to hold the ghatam right and play on it, sit down with it in your lap, with its mouth turned towards your belly, and try hitting it," Luciano explained.

> **!** THE STRINGS OF THE VEENA CAN BE OF BRASS, STEEL, OR EVEN SILVER.

FROM INDIA TO MONGOLIA

It took the cricket and the nightingale several days to get from India to Mongolia, where they were met by a harsh climate, vast steppes, eagle cries, and the howling of wolves in the distance. Who would expect to find music in such an inhospitable place? But Mongolia has a long tradition of composing and playing music.

Fast, go fast! Mongolia is waiting.

THE MORIN KHUUR AND ANIMALS

The music of the morin khuur pleases animals, too. Mongolian nomads, who live in the Gobi Desert, are so in touch with nature that they play the morin khuur to female camels that have just given birth: the deep tones of the instrument have a calming, healing effect on the tired, stressed-out creatures. It is also of great help to camel stepmothers caring for a newborn orphaned following its mother's death.

Where does the beautiful music come from?

MORIN KHUUR

Evidence that rugged Mongolia has an important position in music is provided by the morin khuur, a traditional string instrument that appears on the UNESCO World Heritage List as a symbol of the Mongolian nation. It has a trapezoid wooden body and a head shaped like a horse. The player sounds its two strings by using a bow.

HEAD SHAPED LIKE A HORSE

LEGENDARY ORIGINS OF THE MORIN KHUUR

It is said that many years ago, a Mongolian shepherd received a valuable flying horse as a gift. At night, he would quietly mount this horse and have it carry him in secret to his beloved. But a jealous woman had the horse's wings cut off, so it fell from the sky and died. The unhappy shepherd made the morin khuur from the dead horse's skin and tail, playing the instrument to express his grief.

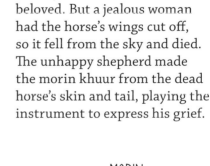

MORIN KHUUR

! **MOST MONGOLIANS** HAVE A MORIN KHUUR AT HOME AS **A SYMBOL OF PEACE AND HAPPINESS.**

OTHER WORLD INSTRUMENTS

Our two music-loving heroes criss-crossed the world, playing, strumming, plucking, banging, and blowing on whatever weird and wonderful instruments crossed their path. In this way, they got to know every musical instrument there has ever been. They took some of them home to play on and as souvenirs.

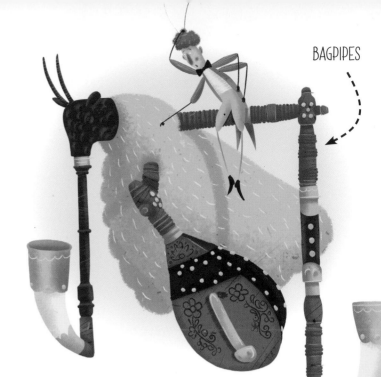

BAGPIPES

BAGPIPES

It's not the bleating of a goat, Niccolo. It's the sound of an ancient musical instrument called the bagpipes. Bagpipes originated as a simple wind instrument in Egypt and the Middle East 4,000 years ago. Nomadic shepherds brought it to Europe, where it established itself very quickly.

SCOTTISH BAGPIPES

On hearing the word bagpipes, most people think first of Scotland. The fact is, however, that this instrument appeared in England in the 13th century, whereas the Scots had to wait for it until the 15th century. It may have taken the Scots a long time to get used to the bagpipes' strange bleating, but they came to enjoy it so much that they have held famous bagpipe competitions since the second half of the 18th century.

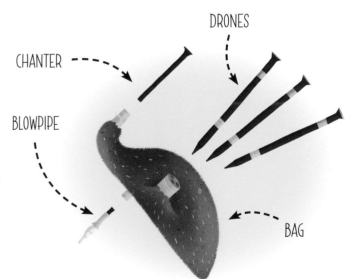

CHANTER
DRONES
BLOWPIPE
BAG

> ! IT IS SAID THAT THERE ARE **AS MANY TYPES** OF BAGPIPES **AS THERE ARE NATIONS.** EACH ONE HAS ADAPTED THE INSTRUMENT TO ITS **OWN TASTES AND NEEDS.**

THREE PARTS, ONE SET OF BAGPIPES

The main part of a set of bagpipes is a blackwood chanter. Then there is the sheepskin windbag, which blows air into the pipe; early bagpipes had an empty wineskin to perform this function. The last part is the drone, which operates as a sound channel. Bagpipes have between one and three drones.

NYCKELHARPA

! THE SWEDISH **POP BAND ABBA** INTRODUCED THE NYCKELHARPA TO **THE WORLD IN THEIR** SONG **DUM DUM DIDDLE.**

NYCKELHARPA

This has a bow and keys. What is it? The six-stringed national instrument of Sweden called the nyckelharpa, of course! Played with a bow, its notes are created by pressing one of 37 keys. Although the oldest picture of the nyckelharpa is from the mid-14th century, it became widely used in the Swedish province of Uppland two centuries later.

BALALAIKA

BALALAIKA

Melancholy tones drifted over the endless Russian plain to the ears of Niccolo the cricket. Luciano the songbird began to warble along to the rhythm. These sounds were coming from a triangular, guitar-like Russian folk instrument called a balalaika, the three strings of which have plucked at the romantic hearts of bold bogatyrs for four centuries.

CONJURING NOTES

"Abracadabra," chants the musician, as he waves a hand mysteriously above a wooden box with two antennae coming from it. The melody that his palm brings forth is almost cosmic-sounding. The upright antenna controls the pitch, the loop antenna the volume. The player does not need to touch the instrument at all. This electronic instrument, called a theremin, was invented in the 1920s by Russian physicist Léon Theremin. As you can see, it's possible to make music on practically anything!

VOZEMBOUCH

VOZEMBOUCH, CAN YOU BLEAT?

Long ago, a poor traveling musician in the Czech lands had to help himself by any means possible. So he took a broom handle, attached a string of dried gut to it, stuck a round pot on its bottom end, grabbed a bow, and started to play. The sound wasn't great. So he added a rattle and some bells and beat it against the ground at regular intervals, thus adding to the weak bleating its distinctive clatter and jangle. Now the musician was pleased with his instrument: it had cost him practically nothing, yet he could make lots of music with it. If you really want to make music, you can do so using absolutely anything!

THEREMIN

ELECTRONIC MUSIC

Computers, synthesizers, theremins, samplers—are these things musical instruments too? Yes, if people play them. Electronic music may be a baby among the musical styles, but it has been around since the 1970s. One of the first electronic bands was Germany's Kraftwerk.

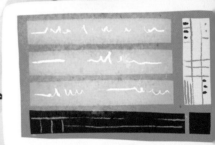

CONCLUSION

Our two ambitious little musicians from the world of crickets and nightingales are back home. But if you think that their long quest for musical instruments has left them any the wiser, you are mistaken, children. Niccolo still doesn't know; Niccolo would like to try everything.

ONE IS ENOUGH

And that's where he's making his mistake! Too many is too much. Put aside five of your six musical toys, Niccolo. One instrument is more than enough to give a person or a cricket a good workout. In the end, Niccolo has decided for the violin—and now he is busy working on the strings, practicing his strokes and scales as well as how to hold the instrument properly. If you want your violin to follow your wishes, every little thing is important.

Do, re, mi, fa, sol, la, ti, do-o-o . . .

VIOLIN AND THE REST . . .

To become a virtuoso musician, meaning one of the very best, you must practice, practice, and practice your instrument. In short, you need to play it for several hours every day. In the belief that he could hold an instrument in each of his limbs, Niccolo chose to play violin, piano, guitar, trumpet, drums, and bagpipes. But oh dear—all that practice was impossible for him to manage!

PLAY WHAT YOU ARE ABLE TO PLAY

And as his dream destination of Carnegie Hall is still very, very far away, Niccolo sometimes invites friends to his home, where he plays on anything he can find there—a washboard, a watering can, drinking glasses, lids, brushes, combs, you name it. In the same way, children, music originated long ago.

CONCERTS

In the evening, the two friends go to concerts and listen carefully to the music. They don't mind if the concert is of classical, rock, jazz, or electronic music. Nor do they mind heavy metal, techno, or folk. All these genres have something to recommend them; all serve to enrich the young musician.

Listen up! I'm si-i-i-inging!

© Designed by B4U Publishing for Albatros, an imprint of Albatros Media Group, 2021.
Na Pankráci 30, Prague 4, Czech Republic
Text by Štěpánka Sekaninová, Illustrations by Jakub Cenkl.
Printed in China by Leo Paper Group.
All rights reserved. Reproduction of any content is strictly prohibited without the written permission of the rights holders.

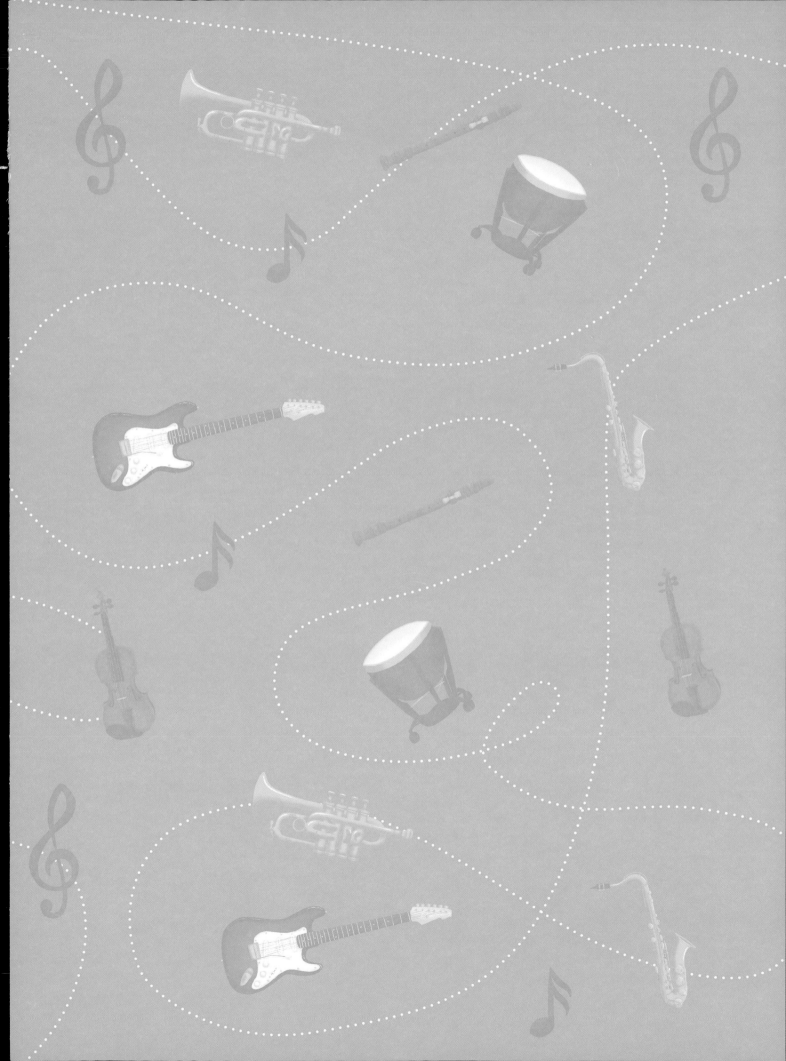

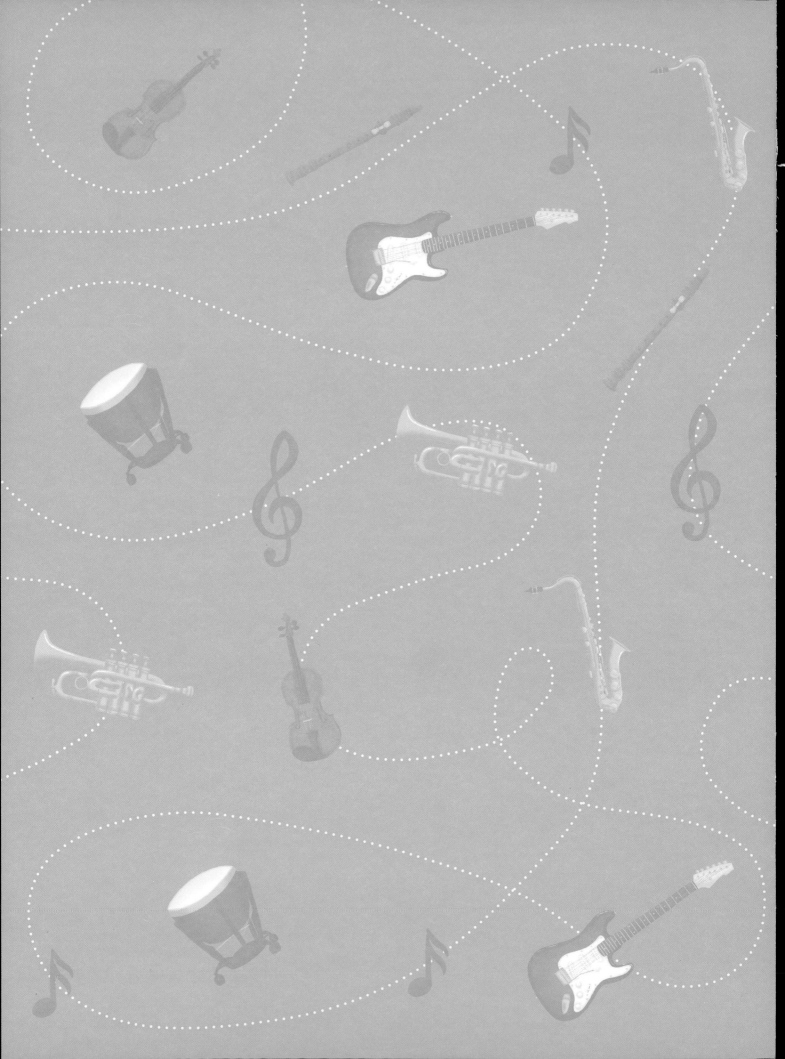